Original title:
A Kaleidoscope of Quiet Chaos

Copyright © 2024 Creative Arts Management OÜ
All rights reserved.

Author: Franklin Stone
ISBN HARDBACK: 978-9916-90-558-6
ISBN PAPERBACK: 978-9916-90-559-3

Kaleidoscopic Echoes of the Unsung

In shadows deep, their voices soar,
Whispers dance on the forgotten floor.
Colors blend in a silent hue,
Echoes call for the hearts anew.

Through tangled dreams, their stories weave,
A symphony born from what we believe.
Mosaic fragments of power unseen,
Hushed anthems rise in the spaces between.

Beneath the stars, their journeys glow,
In every pulse, the unsung know.
Kaleidoscopic in tones so bright,
Shining hopes break the cover of night.

Together they stand, their shadows entwined,
Filling the void, their spirits aligned.
In harmony's embrace, they take flight,
Carving futures from the heart's inner light.

Mosaics of Silence and Urgency

In the hush of night, urgency calls,
Footsteps echo through ancient walls.
Mosaics shine where the dark unfolds,
A tapestry woven of stories untold.

Each breath taken holds stories dear,
A rush of silence, the heart can hear.
The clock ticks loud in the still of hour,
Moments bloom, like a wildflower.

Voices clash in the marketplace loud,
Yet stillness speaks in this restless crowd.
Urgency creeps like a thief in the dark,
While silence hums a forgotten spark.

In every whisper, the world's heartbeat,
Layers of light where chaos and calm meet.
Through the stillness, we find our way,
In mosaics of silence, bright colors sway.

Flickering Thoughts in Peaceful Turmoil

In shadows dance the thoughts that sway,
They flicker bright but fade away.
Amidst the calm, a tempest brews,
In quiet corners, whispers muse.

The heartbeats echo, soft and loud,
Within the silence, thoughts are bowed.
A gentle storm begins to rise,
Beneath the still, the chaos lies.

Moments pass like fleeting dreams,
Caught in the web of silent screams.
Each flicker sparks a hidden fire,
In tranquil night, a deep desire.

Yet in this chaos, peace can find,
A place for solace intertwined.
Embracing all the thoughts that swirl,
In flickering lights, the mind's own pearl.

The Art of Chaotic Silence

In silence hangs a curious art,
Where chaos meets the stillness part.
A canvas blank, yet colors weave,
In quiet depths, the heart believes.

A whisper soft in shadowed night,
Rich with meaning, seeking light.
Expressions buried in the core,
In fragments found, we seek for more.

The rush of thoughts like falling leaves,
Chaotic patterns that the heart weaves.
In stillness loud, a truth unveiled,
In loving silence, hope is hailed.

The echoes heard, though voices cease,
Bring forth a strange and soothing peace.
In chaos held, a quiet grace,
The art of silence finds its place.

Reflections Amidst the Clamor

In bustling streets where voices soar,
Reflections shimmer upon the floor.
A mirror held to fleeting sights,
Where chaos stirs, the soul ignites.

Amidst the noise, a voice rings true,
In clamor bright, a softer hue.
Each glance a story, each face a verse,
In vibrant moments, time's converse.

As laughter fades, and sorrow swells,
In crowded minds, a truth compels.
Each sound a ripple, each pause a thought,
Amidst the clamor, wisdom sought.

Yet in the fray, a calm persists,
A quiet peace that still exists.
Reflections dance despite the storm,
In every chaos, hearts grow warm.

Tides of Subdued Turbulence

Beneath the surface, tides will roll,
Subdued yet wild, they reach the soul.
A wave of thoughts, a pull so strong,
In whispers deep, where echoes throng.

The ocean breathes a restless sigh,
In shifting sands, the secrets lie.
Every swell, a pulse of light,
In subdued waves, the day meets night.

As tempests brew within the heart,
Each crest and trough a work of art.
In silent depths, the calm will break,
With rippling dreams that soon awake.

Yet in this dance, a grace we find,
Tides of turbulence, reassigned.
From chaos born, our strength renews,
In every wave, the journey views.

Echoes of a Turbulent Harmony

Whispers dance through the night air,
A symphony of lost despair.
Notes collide in fleeting flight,
Carrying shadows, chasing light.

Crimson skies, the dawn awakes,
In the silence, the heartbeat breaks.
Harmony woven with heart's regret,
In every echo, a promise met.

Driftwood Dreams and Shattered Silence

Waves crash softly on the shore,
Driftwood tales, forevermore.
Fragments of dreams, washed away,
Lost in the tide, they drift and sway.

Silence shatters with a sigh,
Each moment whispers goodbye.
In the space where shadows play,
Hope lingers, yet fades away.

Fluid Fragments of Serenity

Gentle streams that weave and flow,
In their depths, the secrets glow.
Ripples speak in hushed refrain,
Carving paths through joy and pain.

Bubbles dance on the surface bright,
Mirroring day, mirroring night.
In fluid realms where we both dream,
The soul finds peace, a silent gleam.

Secrets Entwined in a Chaotic Breeze

Leaves flutter in a frantic swirl,
Whispers of a hidden world.
Chaos weaves through every branch,
In laughter, we find our chance.

Dancing shadows, secrets told,
Breezes carry warmth and cold.
In the chaos, love unfolds,
Holding tight to moments bold.

Subdued Crescendo of Clamor

Whispers rise within the crowd,
A hum that swells, then gently bows.
Echoes dance on muted ground,
In shadows where the silence sows.

Faint notes flutter, soft yet bold,
Twinkling lights in dusky haze.
A story in each sigh retold,
In stillness, fervent hearts ablaze.

Pulse of voices, lost, then found,
A melody that breaks the night.
In every pause, a thought profound,
The gentle clash, a tender fight.

Linger in this quiet storm,
Where chaos meets the calm embrace.
A world where dreams begin to form,
In the clamor, find your place.

Hazy Symphony of Tranquil Ruckus

In the distance, laughter swells,
Soft as petals in the breeze.
Sounds entwine like gentle spells,
Nature hums its sweet expertise.

Rustling leaves, a breeze that sighs,
Colorful echoes blend and merge.
Underneath the sunlit skies,
Life's chorus sings, a soothing surge.

Frogs croak softly by the brook,
A rhythm set to nature's beat.
In these moments, time's but a nook,
Where joy and peace serenely meet.

Yet chaos lingers, close but shy,
In the midst of soft delight.
Forever seeking, never I,
A symphony in endless flight.

Dreamscapes of Subtle Turmoil

In twilight realms where shadows grow,
A whisper calls from depths unknown.
Veils of mist, a ghostly show,
Where secrets dwell and seeds are sown.

Drifting softly on the breeze,
Thoughts collide in gentle waves.
In this dance, the heart finds ease,
Chasing echoes, the spirit saves.

Hues of longing shape the night,
Worn paths cross in darker dreams.
Though discord reigns, there's beauty's light,
In turmoil's heart, a spark redeems.

Let the whispers weave their tales,
Between the lines of dusk and dawn.
In tangled threads where chaos hails,
We find the peace that lingers on.

Intricate Harmony in Dissonance

Amidst the clash, a voice emerges,
Layered tones of rich despair.
Different beats, yet spirit surges,
Creating beauty in the air.

Fractured rhythms blend and twine,
Each note a story, rough and raw.
In every moment, there's a sign,
The dissonance holds something more.

Tangled strands of sound unite,
Crafting symphonies from the pain.
In shadows cast, the heart takes flight,
Finding solace in the rain.

Let the discord play its part,
Each echo building, never less.
In intricate paths, we find the art,
Of harmony wrapped in duress.

Intersecting Paths of Stillness

In the quiet woods, whispers breathe,
Branches touch as hearts believe.
Footsteps echo, soft and slow,
Time dances lightly, a gentle flow.

Sunlight filters, a golden thread,
Where shadows linger, silence spread.
Moments pause, the world does sigh,
In stillness found, we learn to fly.

Paths converge, and souls align,
In tranquil spaces, love we find.
A map unwritten in softest hues,
Intersecting paths in quiet views.

Beneath the stars, dreams unfold,
Stories whispered, secrets told.
Here, in this peace, we deeply rest,
Intersecting paths, we are blessed.

The Chaotic Brushstrokes of Calm

Amidst the tempest, colors clash,
Fractured whispers in a flash.
Bold strokes dance, a vibrant tool,
Chaos reigns, yet calm's the rule.

With every drip, a story spills,
Colors collide with untamed thrills.
Swirling thoughts, a canvas wide,
In vibrant disarray, we abide.

A touch of chaos, paint it bright,
Dark and light, both take flight.
In the eye of the storm, peace we find,
Brushstrokes of calm, a masterpiece aligned.

As colors blend, our hearts connect,
In disarray, we sense reflect.
A chaotic dance, yet we stand firm,
With every stroke, we find our term.

Notes from the Edge of Clarity

In whispers faint, the truth is known,
Notes like echoes, softly shown.
Between the lines, the heart confides,
In shadows cast, the clarity hides.

A fleeting thought, like morning dew,
Threads of wisdom, pure and true.
At the edge, the mind takes flight,
Glimmers of dawn break the night.

In silence wrapped, we pause to hear,
The notes that pulse, both far and near.
Beneath the fog, the message glows,
From the edge, the wisdom flows.

Revel in peace, embrace the void,
In notes unplayed, our hearts employed.
At the cusp of light, we dare to dream,
Finding clarity in the unseen.

Colors of Contemplative Mayhem

Chaos rages, wild and free,
In vibrant hues, a swirling sea.
Colors clash and voices raise,
Within the storm, a dance we praise.

In contemplation, we pause awhile,
To trace the lines, to find the smile.
Amidst the clamor, a heartbeat strong,
In beautiful chaos, we belong.

Brushes dipped in thoughts profound,
Creating mayhem all around.
A canvas splashed with joy and pain,
In colors bold, we break the chain.

Lost in beauty, we take a stand,
What seems like chaos, forever planned.
In gentle moments, we unveil,
The colors mixed in contemplative trail.

Hues of Stillness Entwined

In twilight's glow, the shadows sigh,
Whispers of night as the day waves bye.
Colors blend softly in a gentle embrace,
While silence weaves time in a sacred space.

A canvas of dreams painted in grace,
Each brushstroke a memory, a lingering trace.
The stillness captivates, a moment retained,
In hues of tranquility, our hearts are sustained.

The stars emerge, a shy debut,
Glowing above in a palette so true.
Under the heavens, our spirits align,
In the dusk's tender glow, we're eternally fine.

And in this silence, where shadows meet light,
We find our solace in the arms of the night.
Together we linger, forever entwined,
In the hues of stillness, our peace redefined.

The Harmony of Dappled Disorder

In chaos, a rhythm finds its own sway,
Melodies scattered in a bright array.
Nature's wild canvas, untamed and free,
Dancing through shades of what's meant to be.

Leaves flutter down in a raucous flight,
Their whispers echo under the moonlight.
Waves crash ashore with a fervent cheer,
Serenading the night, inviting us near.

Colorful chaos, a beautiful song,
In disorder, we discover what we belong.
Each twinkle, a laugh in the cacophony's heart,
Binding us closer, no need to depart.

So let us embrace this wild symphony,
Where every note resonates, wild and free.
In the harmony of dappled disorder,
We find our rhythm and step closer to order.

Gentle Tempest Beneath the Surface

Beneath the calm lies a stirring storm,
Whispers of winds in a softening form.
Ripples run deep, currents intertwine,
An ocean of feelings, both fierce and divine.

Clouds gather round, a playful tease,
Rumbles of passion that flutter like leaves.
A heartbeat lurking beneath tranquil waves,
In the silent depths, true courage paves.

The beauty of conflict, the strength to endure,
Emerging through struggles, resilient and pure.
For even in tempests, there's grace to be found,
In the gentle currents, our hope knows no bounds.

So ride the tides with a heart full of trust,
Embrace the storms, for they are a must.
In the gentle tempest, we learn to survive,
Finding our essence, awakening alive.

Tangles of Calm and Clamor

In the bustling streets where silence is rare,
Voices collide, filling the air.
Each heartbeat a note in the city's song,
Where calm and clamor together belong.

Amidst the chaos, a moment to breathe,
Finding stillness in layers beneath.
The laughter of children, a sweet serenade,
Amidst sirens and echoes, peace is laid.

In tangled threads, life intertwines,
Weaving soft whispers through fervent designs.
Finding our way in the swirl and the spin,
With every encounter, the journey begins.

So here in the blend, our spirits ignite,
In the calm of the clamor, we find our light.
With hearts intertwined, we dance in this weave,
In the tangles of life, we endlessly believe.

The Sublime Mess of Solitude

In the quiet depths I find,
Thoughts cascade like whispers soft.
Shadows dance, memories entwined,
In solitude, I learn to loft.

Time stretches thin like fragile thread,
A tapestry of dreams unsown.
In this vastness, hope is fed,
Embracing what I've never known.

But beauty weaves through empty air,
Each breath a gift, each sigh a song.
In the stillness, I feel fair,
Finding where my heart belongs.

The stars above begin to glow,
Illuminating paths unseen.
In solitude, I learn to grow,
For in the mess, I'm truly keen.

Chaos Wrapped in Gentle Moments

Storms rage softly in the night,
Fury cloaked in velvet hues.
Birds take flight at dawn's first light,
In chaos, life finds vibrant cues.

Gentle laughter breaks the norm,
Amidst the frenzy, hearts entwine.
In every tempest, there's a charm,
A dance of fate, a sacred sign.

With every whisper of the breeze,
The wild toll of nature calls.
Yet in the madness, there's a peace,
A balance in the rise and falls.

Embrace the whirlwind, feel the rush,
In tender moments, truth unfolds.
For chaos blooms, a powerful hush,
In gentle hands, the world beholds.

Chimeras of Silence and Noise

In echoes where shadows dwell,
Silence speaks the loudest tune.
Chimeras weave their secret spell,
In twilight's glow, beneath the moon.

Voices whisper from the dark,
A dance of thoughts, a haunting play.
Within the stillness, there's a spark,
That leads the heart to drift away.

Yet noise cascades like rushing streams,
Clattering dreams that shape the day.
In the chaos, truth redeems,
Both silence and sound in grand ballet.

A symphony of blend, not one,
In every pulse, the world ignites.
Chimeras thrive till day is done,
In harmony, they share their sights.

Twisted Serenades of the Mind

Thoughts spiral like a winding vine,
Whispers tracing edges blurred.
In the labyrinth, suns align,
A serenade, yet unencurred.

Faces of fears in shadows play,
Reflections lost, then found anew.
In reverie of night and day,
The heart unveils what's always true.

Melodies of joy and strife,
Compose the music of the soul.
Each note reveals the dance of life,
The twisted paths that make us whole.

In mind's embrace, the stories flow,
A symphony of hope and grief.
In every turn, the seeds we sow,
Craft twisted serenades, our belief.

Fragmented Dreams

In shadows deep, the whispers sigh,
A tapestry where visions lie.
Mosaic pieces, splintered light,
Chasing echoes through the night.

Fractured hopes in scattered hues,
A dance of colors, lost in views.
Fleeting moments slip away,
As dawn breaks on a broken day.

Coalescing Colors

Brush of twilight paints the sky,
Crimson dreams and sapphire sighs.
Golden rays begin to blend,
Unity in hues, a splendid mend.

Violet whispers, emerald gleam,
In this palette, life's a dream.
Each stroke connects the heart and mind,
In the canvas, hope we find.

The Underlying Pulse of Pandemonium

Chaos swirls in vibrant dance,
An orchestra caught in chance.
Heartbeats echo in the fray,
Pulsing life in disarray.

Voices rise, then intertwine,
Fractured notes in wild design.
A symphony of joy and pain,
In every chaos, beauty reigns.

Shattered Reflections

In the mirror, shards of grace,
Fragments of a forgotten place.
Each piece holds a sacred story,
Tales of loss wrapped in glory.

Glimmers dance in fractured light,
Wounds that heal but still invite.
Through the break, the truth prevails,
Finding self within the veils.

Quiet Thoughts

In tranquil moments, silence speaks,
Thoughts meander like gentle creeks.
Soft reflections in the still,
Whispers linger, hearts to fill.

Each breath a pause, a gift of peace,
In solitude, the mind's release.
Calm descends like evening's cloak,
In quietude, wisdom's woke.

Diversions within the Calm

Beneath the surface, ripples play,
Diverse paths we tread each day.
In still waters, subtle shifts,
Hidden treasures, the spirit lifts.

Nature's whispers call us near,
Inviting hearts to pause and hear.
In every choice, a dance unfolds,
In calm, the story softly told.

Whispers in the Wardrobe

In shadows deep, secrets dwell,
Fabric folds where dreams compel,
A hush that speaks, soft and clear,
In the dark, it draws us near.

Old coats sigh like ancient tales,
Faded voices ride the gales,
Each thread tells of love and loss,
In this space, we bear the cross.

The scent of dust, a memory's kiss,
Timeless whispers, the secrets we miss,
Through ticking clocks, the moments weave,
In the wardrobe, we dare to believe.

When night unfolds its velvet drape,
We listen close for escape,
In quiet corners, we find our way,
Whispers in the wardrobe, come what may.

Fractured Echoes of Stillness

A shattered silence fills the room,
Where shadows dance, and heartbeats loom,
Each breath a mark of time's cruel test,
In stillness wrapped, we seek our rest.

The echoes speak in fractured tones,
Of whispered fears and broken bones,
Here lies the weight of dreams undone,
In quivering light, the battle's won.

Moments linger, then drift away,
In the calm, we start to sway,
Each echo fades but leaves a trace,
In quietude, we find our place.

A pause that hangs like morning dew,
In fractured echoes, we find the true,
For in stillness, we face the night,
And emerge reborn in dawn's soft light.

Choreography of Silent Storms

In swirling winds, the silence shatters,
As whispers rise, the heartbeat matters,
Footsteps echo in the darkened haze,
A ballet born of tempestuous ways.

Unseen forces reign and collide,
In this dance, we cannot hide,
Every flicker lights the way,
Choreographed in shades of gray.

Waves of quiet, a thunderous call,
In chaos found, we stand tall,
With every storm, we learn to bend,
A story crafted with no end.

As lightning strikes, we find our grace,
In silent storms, we carve our space,
And when the eye reveals the calm,
We rise anew, our souls like balm.

Tapestry of Unseen Whirls

In threads of light, nightmares intertwine,
A tapestry of dreams divine,
Each color spun from hopes concealed,
In unseen whirls, our truths revealed.

The fabric whispers of tales untold,
In woven wonders, we break the mold,
With every twist, a journey begins,
In sources deep, where love transcends.

A dance of pattern, a sacred art,
In fragile moments, we play our part,
Through the loom of life, we stitch our fates,
In unseen whirls, the heart elates.

Threads may fray, yet beauty thrives,
In the tapestry, our spirit strives,
For in each layer, we find the whole,
In unseen whirls, we touch the soul.

Crescendo of Hidden Anxieties

In shadows where thoughts softly creep,
Whispers of dread, they softly seep.
The heart beats fast, a thunderous sound,
Amidst the silence, fears abound.

Thoughts taut like strings, ready to snap,
In the stillness, I find my trap.
Echoes of worries in the night,
Crescendo rises, fears take flight.

Daylight breaks, a fragile mask,
Hiding the burden, a daunting task.
Yet, beneath the smile, shadows play,
Anxieties dance, they won't stay away.

But every storm will find its calm,
Amidst the chaos, there lies a balm.
In the depths, I seek the light,
A symphony of peace ignites the night.

The Balance of Fragile Frenzy

In the whirlwind of daily strife,
A delicate dance of chaotic life.
Every heartbeat, a swing and sway,
In search of balance, I find my way.

Thoughts collide, like waves on shore,
Tugging at me, forevermore.
Yet in the chaos, strength I glean,
A fragile frenzy, yet serene.

Moments flutter, like leaves they fall,
Caught in rapture, I heed the call.
With every breath, a choice to make,
To find my peace, or break awake.

In the stillness, I mend and weave,
Finding solace in what I believe.
The balance held in gentle hands,
A fragile dance, as life expands.

Unruly Blossoms in Gentle Quiet

In the garden where wildflowers bloom,
Colors burst forth, dispelling gloom.
Petals unfurl in a riotous way,
Unruly blossoms, come what may.

In gentle quiet, their beauty sings,
A melody of unspoken things.
Yet in their freedom, lies a trace,
Of chaos wrapped in nature's grace.

Whispers of wind, a soft embrace,
Carrying secrets, a tender space.
In every flower, life finds a way,
Unruly blossoms, brightening the day.

Among the stillness, joy takes root,
Amidst the wild, there lies the truth.
In their dance, I find my heart,
Unruly blossoms, a work of art.

Bursts of Solitude's Splendor

In the hush of dawn, soft light blooms,
A silent symphony in empty rooms.
Each moment stretches, a tapestry spun,
In solitude's splendor, I find the sun.

Thoughts ripple out, like a still pond,
In deep reflections, I feel so fond.
Bursts of clarity, whispers of peace,
In quiet corners, my worries cease.

Time lingers here, an eternal sigh,
Moments embraced, as day drifts by.
In solitude's arms, I'm never alone,
Splendor unfolds, a heart's true home.

Every breath fills the space I keep,
In solitude's splendor, my spirit leaps.
Embracing the still, I learn to be,
Awake in the world, yet lost in me.

Tranquil Unraveling of Thought

In the silence of the night,
Whispers dance in soft delight.
Moonlight drapes the restless dreams,
Caught in gentle, flowing streams.

Thoughts like petals slowly fall,
Crimson hints against the wall.
Each unfolding a new clue,
To the heart, both pure and true.

In the stillness, time stands still,
Softly breathing, bend to will.
Quiet echoes, a cosmic play,
Soothe the mind, melt fears away.

Here, in peace, the world expands,
Finding light in empty hands.
In the void, a vibrant spark,
Guides us gently through the dark.

Shadows of Serenity and Sound

In the shade of whispering trees,
Softly sung by the evening breeze.
Echoes linger, secrets shared,
A tranquil world, gently declared.

Rippling waters soothe the night,
Moonlit paths, a silver light.
Harmony is all around,
In the stillness, peace is found.

Shadows weave a calming thread,
Through the whispers softly spread.
Nature's chorus, pure and sweet,
Cradles hearts in rhythmic beat.

In the embrace of dusk's embrace,
We find solace, find our place.
A gentle lull, a warm goodbye,
As stars awaken in the sky.

Threads of Vibrant Whispers

Colors dance in twilight's hue,
Every whisper feels like new.
Threads of laughter weave the night,
Binding dreams with purest light.

Let the echoes softly flow,
In the dark, let spirits glow.
Voices blend, a tapestry,
Woven close in harmony.

Gentle breezes carry sound,
Carving moments all around.
In the quiet, hearts align,
Every breath a sacred sign.

Through the fabric of our days,
Vibrant whispers craft the ways.
In our stories, love will thrive,
As long as we remain alive.

The Pulse of Unwritten Stories

In the canvas of the night,
Unwritten tales take flight.
Every heartbeat, every sigh,
Fills the darkened, endless sky.

Dreams and wishes softly blend,
In the silence, paths extend.
Each unwritten word awaits,
Life's embrace, the hand of fate.

Moments linger, whispers call,
Echoes rise and gently fall.
In the shadows, truths align,
Sculpting fate, divine design.

With each breath, the stories bloom,
Painting light from hints of gloom.
As we journey, let us learn,
The heart's pulse will always yearn.

The Dance of Dissonant Dreams

In shadows where the whispers blend,
Echoes of laughter begin to bend.
Colors bleed in twisted light,
Fractured visions take to flight.

Hearts collide in silent screams,
Chasing down elusive dreams.
A waltz of chaos, dark yet bright,
Melding darkness with the light.

Steps unsteady, rhythm lost,
Every beat a heavy cost.
Yet in discord, beauty lies,
A symphony beneath the skies.

Through the noise, a song will rise,
Filling voids with hidden sighs.
In the dance, we find our place,
In dissonance, a shared embrace.

Vibrant Fragments in Stillness

Between the breaths of a quiet dawn,
Colors shimmer with a gentle yawn.
Every silence tells a tale,
Whispers carved in the morning pale.

Petals fall in soft descent,
Nature's canvas, a pure intent.
Each hue sings a forgotten song,
In stillness, where the heart belongs.

Time stands still, a fleeting glance,
Caught within this sacred dance.
Fragments of life like shattered glass,
Reflect the moments hard to pass.

In the echoes, memories wane,
Yet vibrant threads still remain.
Embrace the stillness, let it flow,
In every pause, the colors glow.

Murmurs of the Unseen Whirl

Between the stars and timeless night,
Whispers twirl in gentle flight.
Hidden realms of silent grace,
Dancing dreams in twilight's lace.

Voices linger on the breeze,
Murmurs drift through ancient trees.
In the dark, a soft refrain,
Hints of joy wrapped in pain.

Cascades of light through shadows fall,
Mysteries beckon, softly call.
In the unseen, secrets unfold,
Stories waiting to be told.

Through the stillness, hear the sound,
Of life's magic all around.
In this whirl, both fierce and kind,
In every murmur, truth you'll find.

Serenity in a Twisting Storm

As thunder rumbles, shadows loom,
A tempest brews, the air's in gloom.
Yet within, a calm resides,
A peaceful heart where chaos hides.

Winds like voices twist and weave,
Nature's dance in a grand reprieve.
Lightning flashes, illuminating night,
In turmoil, finds a quiet light.

The world spins in a frenzied pass,
But serenity forms like glass.
In the eye of storms, stillness reigns,
Where hope and strength break all chains.

So let the storm rage, wild and bold,
In every gust, a story told.
For in the chaos, peace can bloom,
Serenity shines, dispelling gloom.

Stillness Beneath the Raging Sea

Beneath the waves, calm shadows sweep,
Where secrets of the deep still sleep.
The surface dances, wild and free,
Yet silence reigns in depths we see.

A whisper calls from ocean's heart,
Amidst the storm, it plays its part.
The world above can roar and rage,
While quiet rests, a hidden stage.

In currents soft, time seems to pause,
Life flickers gently, just because.
The chaos churns, but here we find,
A tranquil peace, a soothing mind.

So when the tempests storm our way,
Remember stillness, come what may.
For in the depths, where waters flow,
The heart finds rest, and calm can grow.

Hidden Currents of Gentle Chaos

In every wave, a story flows,
Riding currents no one knows.
Beneath the tide, soft eddies spin,
A dance of whispers, where dreams begin.

The frothy crest belies the peace,
While gentle pulls grant sweet release.
A world below, so rich, unseen,
Holds subtle truths, serene and keen.

Each ripple tells a tale of grace,
Of hidden paths in water's embrace.
For chaos lurks in stillness' hands,
In gentle currents where hope stands.

Amid the turmoil, we shall find,
The beauty rests in heart and mind.
For every storm that shakes our core,
Leaves room for calm to rise once more.

Flickers of Calm in the Tempest

When thunder rolls and skies grow dark,
A flicker shines, a tiny spark.
In wildest storms, a light prevails,
Guiding souls through tempest's wails.

The winds may howl, the waters churn,
Yet here the heart will softly yearn.
For in the chaos, calm does dwell,
A treasured peace, a sacred spell.

Each raindrop falls, a whispered song,
In rhythm, where we all belong.
The storm may rage, but we can see,
A flicker glows, a clarity.

So hold that light within your chest,
Embrace the chaos, find your rest.
For amidst the fury, we shall find,
A beacon bright, forever aligned.

Unseen Kaleidoscopic Whirlpools

In swirling depths, colors entwine,
A dance of hues, serene, divine.
Kaleidoscope of chaos, grand,
In secret waters, dreams expand.

Whirlpools pull with gentle might,
A spiral down, a wondrous sight.
Invisible paths, they weave and wind,
The beauty hidden from the blind.

Their essence flows, a vibrant stream,
Where thoughts dissolve and shadows gleam.
In every twist, a new embrace,
Reflecting life, a fluid grace.

So linger long where currents swirl,
Explore the depths of this bright world.
For in each whirl, a chance to see,
The unseen beauty, wild and free.

Murmurs among the Fray

In corners where whispers softly collide,
A tapestry woven with secrets unspied.
Voices like shadows, in twilight they play,
Unraveling stories as night turns to day.

Footsteps echo in a dance of the lost,
Each heartbeat a signal, no matter the cost.
In silence we gather, in chaos we thrive,
Murmurs igniting the spark to survive.

In the midst of the frenzy, a calmness appears,
An undercurrent flowing beneath all the fears.
Through laughter and sorrow, we weave a new thread,
Murmurs of promise where once there was dread.

Like tendrils of smoke, we rise and we bend,
Finding a solace where cacophony ends.
In whispers of comfort, we locate our way,
Murmurs among the fray, forever we'll stay.

Shadows Dancing in Disorder

In the flicker of light, they twist and they sway,
A banquet of chaos, in wild disarray.
Each movement a story, each shadow a friend,
Dancing through darkness, where echoes transcend.

Beneath the moon's gaze, they whirl through the night,
A ballet of shadows, elusive and light.
With laughter as music, they pirouette free,
Lost in the rhythm of unyielding glee.

Though tangled and wild, there's beauty profound,
In each fleeting moment, a joy to be found.
Amidst wild confusion, they waltz with delight,
Shadows dancing in disorder, a magical sight.

In uncharted realms where the unexpected roams,
These shadows unite to find warmth in their homes.
Together they shimmer, they flicker, they soar,
In a world full of strife, they offer much more.

Patterns of Hushed Turbulence

Ripples unseen in a pond of still grace,
Murmurs of energy fill up the space.
Each heartbeat a rhythm, a pattern we weave,
Hushed turbulence whispers, it's harder to leave.

Moments of stillness, then bursts of delight,
Chaos that lingers just out of our sight.
In the quietest corners, where shadows reside,
Patterns emerge like the shifting of tides.

Through layers of silence, we unearth our path,
Navigating fissures where calm meets the wrath.
In the interplay woven, the dance of the wild,
Hushed turbulence beckons, our heartbeats compiled.

Each sigh tells a story, each breath shares a name,
A tapestry woven, unbroken by shame.
In patterns of whispers, we find our embrace,
Hushed turbulence cradles the echoes of grace.

The Art of Gentle Mayhem

In every soft whisper, a tempest brews bright,
The art of gentle mayhem unfolds in the night.
With laughter like ripples, we stir up the calm,
Each riotous heartbeat, a soft, soothing balm.

Chaos in colors, a palette so wide,
Imperfect yet splendid, where wonders abide.
Dancing through moments, both fragile and bold,
The art of gentle mayhem, a tale to be told.

In unity found through a glorious mess,
Every tangle of life, an intricate dress.
Celebrating whispers that dare to be loud,
The art of creation, defying the crowd.

As light meets the laughter, we bask in the shine,
Blurring the edges from yours into mine.
In every small chaos, a reason to sway,
The art of gentle mayhem, our hearts on display.

Broken Mirrors in Serene Waters

In waters deep, reflections lie,
Fragments of dreams that once could fly.
Ripples dance on glassy blue,
Echoes of whispers, the past in view.

Beneath the veil, truths intertwine,
Mirrored pieces of heart and time.
Serenity blends with shards of pain,
A beauty born from the broken chain.

Gazing within, the soul takes flight,
Lost in the shadows, found in the light.
Each glance reveals a story told,
In tranquil corners, secrets unfold.

What once was whole, now tells a tale,
Of battles fought, yet spirits prevail.
In stillness, whispers unlock the door,
To the depths of what we were before.

The Stillness in the Heart of Madness

Beneath the chaos, silence breathes,
A stillness woven through tangled weaves.
In minds that race, a quiet call,
To find the peace that breaks the fall.

Amidst the fray, thoughts start to swirl,
A dance of chaos, an unending whirl.
Yet in the eye, a calm prevails,
A soothing balm when the tempest wails.

The heart beats fierce, yet tempered slow,
In whispered moments, the truth will show.
Madness sings in its wildest tune,
While stillness waits, a quiet boon.

In shadows deep, light gently creeps,
Awakens the silence, where stillness sleeps.
In the heart of chaos, wisdom finds,
The tranquil mind that gently binds.

Hushed Roars of Life's Complexity

In silence loud, the world unfolds,
A symphony where life beholds.
Layers twist in harmonic design,
A canvas painted with threads divine.

Whispers echo in vibrant hues,
Complexities born from varied views.
From laughter bright to shadows long,
Each story woven is part of the song.

Every heartbeat a narrative spun,
In woven tales, we are all one.
The hush of chaos, a paradox clear,
For in our silence, we truly hear.

With every sigh, the cosmos breathes,
In each embrace, the mind receives.
The world around, a dance of grace,
In hushed roars, we find our place.

Spectrum of Quiet Disturbances

In the quiet, colors swirl,
A spectrum bright as dreams unfurl.
Each shade a whisper, soft yet clear,
Of hidden truths that linger near.

Subtle shifts in the light we see,
Creating waves of mystery.
Where silence treads, the heart can quake,
In gentle tremors, new paths we make.

Through unseen hues, emotions glide,
In depth of quiet, we often hide.
Yet every pulse brings forth a change,
Disturbances silent, yet vast and strange.

As daylight fades, the spectrum sighs,
In quiet moments, our spirit flies.
Exploring realms where silence reigns,
In the heart of stillness, our freedom gains.

Soft Revolutions of the Mind

In the quiet dusk of thought,
Ideas softly drift and sway,
Whispers of dreams begin to dance,
In the shadows where night holds sway.

Moments flutter like bright leaves,
Colors merge in gentle streams,
Every doubt begins to fade,
Replaced by the birth of dreams.

As thoughts unwind and intertwine,
Patterns emerge in soft embrace,
Revolutions within the mind,
In a still and sacred space.

New worlds form in twilight's hush,
Where calm and chaos intertwine,
Embracing all that life can give,
In soft revolutions, we align.

Veils of Calm in the Whirlwind

Within the storm, a secret peace,
Veils of calm, they twist and twirl,
Cocooned in silence, hearts ignite,
Amidst the chaos, dreams unfurl.

The winds may howl and earth may shake,
Yet stillness blooms, a fragile flower,
Caught in the eye, a moment's grace,
Time slows down, and we empower.

Colors catch in flying debris,
Yet deep within the heart a light,
Guides through the noise, the spinning fate,
Creating calm in endless night.

Veils of calm in the whirlwind dance,
Transforming dread to sweet embrace,
In every tempest, a chance to find,
Serenity's gentle face.

Serene Disarray

In tangled thoughts, a beauty lies,
Whispers mix with dreams set free,
Colors clash in vibrant ways,
Creating art in disarray.

Moments stitched with loose thread,
Frayed edges tell our secret tales,
Harmonies arise from chaos,
A symphony where balance fails.

The world spins on, a dizzy dance,
In every swirl, new visions bloom,
Finding solace in the noise,
Creating life within the gloom.

Serene disarray, our guiding star,
Navigates through shadows cast,
A testament to what we've found,
In chaos, peace holds steadfast.

Whispers of Controlled Chaos

In the heartbeat of the night,
Where shadows play and spirits roam,
Whispers tease the edges close,
Chaos knows us, calls us home.

With careful hands, we shape our fate,
Dancing lightly on the strings,
Juggling dreams, fears intertwined,
In this game of fragile things.

A laughter echoes in the void,
Melodies pierce the fabric thin,
Every flaw a brushstroke bold,
On the canvas, life begins.

Crafting moments, threading light,
Whispers weave through chaos, free,
Controlled yet wild, we find our song,
In the whispers, we discover we.

Soft Cries of a Wandering Mind

In the hush of night, thoughts take flight,
Whispers of dreams, elusive and bright.
A gentle sigh drifts with the breeze,
Lost in a maze, seeking sweet ease.

Fleeting moments of clarity,
Echoing softly their rarity.
Heart's soft beat, a lullaby,
Cocooned in shadows, where secrets lie.

Paths intertwine in twilight's glow,
Shimmering visions of tales untold.
Each step a puzzle, a chance to find,
The soft cries echo of a wandering mind.

Patterns in the Pandemonium

Amidst the chaos, a rhythm plays,
Colors collide in vibrant arrays.
The dance of shadows, a fierce embrace,
Forming a tapestry, a wild chase.

Rushing waters, a tempest roars,
Yet in the storm, a pattern soars.
Lines intertwine in a frantic spree,
Artistry born from entropy.

Fragments of noise create a song,
Each note, a heartbeat, where we belong.
In the pandemonium, visions align,
Discovering patterns, both bold and divine.

Emotion's Colorful Subtlety

With a stroke of light, feelings emerge,
Gentle hues blend, a tranquil verge.
Soft pastels whisper, secrets in sight,
While vibrant shades dance in pure delight.

Each emotion, a canvas, broad and wide,
Through quiet brushstrokes, we choose to hide.
Tender smiles hold stories untold,
In this colorful tapestry, hearts unfold.

Melancholy blues, a soulful thread,
Joy's blazing yellows where hope is bred.
In the palette of life, find your own hue,
In subtlety's embrace, let feelings be true.

The Symphony of Quiet Whirlwinds

Whirlwinds whisper through an open field,
Creating a symphony that's gently sealed.
Rustling leaves, a delicate song,
In the quiet dance where we belong.

Breath of nature in tender spins,
Carrying tales of where it begins.
Softly swirling in hushed delight,
Painting the dusk with whispers bright.

Notes of the world, both loud and meek,
Intertwined melodies, together they speak.
In the stillness, a storm takes flight,
The symphony swells in the depths of the night.

A Tapestry of Silent Contrasts

Colors blend in quiet night,
Each hue whispers tales of light.
In shadows linger dreams untold,
A canvas rich, both soft and bold.

The sun dips low, the stars ignite,
A symphony of dark and bright.
Dualities in gentle grace,
Unraveled threads in time and space.

Eyes perceive what hearts can't say,
In silence, worlds seem far away.
Yet every heartbeat, every sigh,
Weaves a story, never shy.

So in this weave of what we feel,
The silent contrasts slowly heal.
Embrace the tapestry we share,
Together, woven with great care.

Unraveled Patterns of Inner Sound

Echoes ripple through the mind,
Each layer rich, each thought entwined.
Voices linger in the air,
A dance of sound that strips us bare.

Unraveled threads of whispers fall,
In solitude, we hear the call.
Patterns shift, then fade away,
Leaving traces of yesterday.

The heart beats loud in tranquil space,
Navigating through time's embrace.
Melodies of lost refrain,
Resound within the quiet's gain.

So find the harmony inside,
In the silence, let it guide.
Listen close, and you may find,
The hidden truths that intertwine.

The Soft Collision of Ideas

Thoughts collide like gentle rain,
Droplets falling, washed of pain.
In the chaos, sparks ignite,
A dance of concepts takes its flight.

Fragments merge, then split apart,
Creating maps within the heart.
Ideas swirl in vibrant blend,
A tapestry without an end.

Each notion whispers, seeks to grow,
In fertile ground where dreams may flow.
The brush of minds, a tender blaze,
Ignites the night in subtle ways.

Embrace the chaos, let it swell,
In every riddle, stories dwell.
Together we can build anew,
In soft collisions, seek the true.

Whispered Dances of Fragile Life

Life unfurls in whispered tones,
Each moment sings, but rarely moans.
Fragile steps on tender ground,
In fleeting grace, our joys are found.

The elegance of every breath,
A dance that flirts with life and death.
In shadows cast by fleeting light,
We find the strength to face the night.

Soulful touches, soft and clear,
Moving closer, chasing fear.
In rhythm's pulse, we all connect,
The fragile weave we can protect.

So let us dance through joy and strife,
In whispered steps, embrace this life.
Together, we will laugh and sigh,
In fragile beauty, love won't die.

Silent Whirlwinds of Thought

Whispers dance in the night air,
Thoughts swirl like leaves in despair.
Echoes drift, lost in the breeze,
Silent moments, time's gentle tease.

Memories linger, shadows align,
Curved reflections, paths intertwine.
Within the mind, chaos and calm,
Finding solace, a subtle balm.

Winds of change whisper their names,
In the silence, the heart still flames.
Questions rise, like stars in the sky,
Breaking free, letting worries fly.

In the quiet, a journey begins,
Through the storms, beneath the skin.
Whirlwinds of thought, unbound and true,
In this silence, I find the new.

Threads of Dissonant Peace

Tangled strings in a desperate weave,
Pieces hidden, few will believe.
Harmony lost in a fractal scheme,
Searching for the elusive dream.

Colors clash, yet softly blend,
A canvas raw, where edges bend.
Amidst the noise, a tranquil sigh,
Dissonance sings, yet we still try.

Whispers of hope in every scar,
Seeking light from the distant star.
In chaos, a heartbeat remains,
Threads of peace, amid the pains.

Embrace the chaos, let it flow,
Harmony blooms where wild winds blow.
Find the stillness in every crease,
In dissonance, we find our peace.

Vibrations within Silent Echoes

Gentle ripples in a boundless space,
Silent echoes, a soft embrace.
Vibrations pulse, though unseen,
Carving paths where we have been.

Every whisper, a tale unfolds,
Hidden stories that silence holds.
In the void, there's a tender grace,
Vibrations dance in quiet place.

Stillness speaks in a thousand ways,
Guiding hearts through the darkest days.
In echoes soft, we find our sound,
Vibrations lift from the underground.

Listen closely, let your soul roam,
In silent echoes, we find our home.
The world vibrates, beneath our feet,
In every silence, the pulse is sweet.

The Silent Roar of Unraveled Dreams

In whispers deep, a thunder wakes,
Unraveled dreams, the heart now shakes.
Quiet chaos in the night,
Beyond the dark, a flickering light.

The silent roar of hopes untold,
Visions painted in colors bold.
In stillness, futures start to gleam,
Awakening from the deepest dream.

Time ticks softly, yet speaks so loud,
In every heartbeat, I'm unbowed.
Unraveled threads, a tapestry grand,
In silent roars, I take a stand.

With each moment, a wave of grace,
Rebuilding worlds in this sacred space.
From disruptions, I learn to fly,
The silent roar, my spirit's cry.

The Intersection of Calm and Clatter

In the midst of noise, a whisper sighs,
Waves of distraction, beneath clear skies.
Gentle moments pause the frantic race,
Finding solace in an empty space.

Clattering plates, laughter intertwines,
A soft melody where tension reclines.
Footsteps echo, yet hearts beat slow,
At this junction, peace begins to grow.

Between chaos and stillness, balance sways,
Finding grace in the wildest of plays.
Hushed conversations weave through the loud,
In this harmony, we are unbowed.

So here's to the calm among the din,
Where the battle of silence begins to thin.
In every uproar, there's a chance to find,
The intersection where hearts unwind.

Mysterious Patterns in the Quiet

Nightfall blankets the world in peace,
A canvas of silence where wonders increase.
Stars entangle tales in soft woven threads,
Whispers of secrets where the stillness spreads.

Beneath the moon's glow, shadows softly dance,
Patterns emerge in a twilight trance.
Each breath a story, every heartbeat slow,
In the depths of quiet, mysteries flow.

Clouds drift lazily, dreams take flight,
In the hug of tranquility, hidden delights.
Echoes of thought surface with ease,
Crafting a language known only to trees.

The secret's embrace, a soft lullaby,
Underneath the calm, the unseen will fly.
In every corner of stillness confide,
The patterns of life where wonders abide.

Resonance of Chaos Beneath Stillness

Like thunder rumbling beyond the calm,
The heart beats fierce, yet seeking balm.
In whispered moments, the tempest hides,
Underneath veneer, the wildness bides.

The world spins round in a meteor's blaze,
Where chaos breathes in a vibrant haze.
Each rustle and shiver, a song of the free,
Echoing loudly in the shadows of me.

Through stillness we harness the raging tide,
Embracing the conflict, there's nowhere to hide.
In quiet reflection, storms come alive,
Concealing within what we know will survive.

From chaos to peace, the journey is clear,
Each moment we gather, we hold it near.
In stillness, listen; there's music so bold,
The resonance reveals what remains untold.

The Artistry of Intricate Disorder

A canvas of chaos, colors collide,
In tangled brushstrokes, emotions abide.
Unruly patterns dance with delight,
In the heart of the tempest, art takes flight.

Fragments of laughter, splattered with tears,
The beauty of life framed by its fears.
Every sharp angle, a story to tell,
In the craftsmanship woven, we find ourselves well.

Twists and turns in a rhythmic embrace,
Where imperfections create the space.
Every misstep sings with vibrant grace,
In the chaos of life, we find our place.

So cherish the chaos, the chaos of dreams,
Each vivid misalignment bursting at seams.
For in intricate disorder, there's art to behold,
A masterpiece woven in colors so bold.

The Stillness After the Storm

Whispers linger in the air,
Softly brushing trees and ground.
The clouds part, revealing sky,
As silence wraps the world around.

Puddles mirror fading light,
A dance of droplets on the grass.
Nature breathes, a calm reprieve,
In stillness, moments come to pass.

Birdsong breaks the heavy hush,
Each note like a gentle touch.
Hope blooms where water pooled,
From chaos, life emerges much.

Now the sun begins to rise,
Embers warm the cool terrain.
In the aftermath we find,
A world renewed, free from pain.

Harmonizing Fragments of Chaos

In shadows dance the fragments lost,
Scattered thoughts in restless night.
A symphony of clashing dreams,
Each note pulls at heartstrings tight.

Windswept thoughts begin to merge,
While starlight weaves a golden thread.
Through chaos, patterns start to form,
As melodies awaken dread.

Voices intertwine, emerge as one,
In harmony, they rise and swell.
From disarray, a truth takes flight,
In fractured tales, we weave our spell.

The fragments sing, a wild refrain,
Bringing solace to the strife.
In this chaos, we find our way,
A map of dreams, a dance of life.

Radiant Contradictions in Quietude

Silent smiles beneath the veil,
A paradox that softly glows.
In quiet moments, hearts collide,
Where light and shadow intertwine like prose.

The laughter echoes in the dark,
Shining bright amidst the gloom.
In stillness dwells a vibrant spark,
A testament to what may bloom.

Each breath a whisper, a soft sigh,
Contradiction wrapped in grace.
For in the calm, turmoil may lie,
Yet beauty finds its rightful place.

Embrace the light, the dark, the in-between,
Where calm and chaos gently meet.
In every truth, a doubled scene,
Radiant heartbeats, bittersweet.

Quiet Floods of Euphoria

Gentle waves of bliss cascade,
Washing over weary minds.
Each drop a thrill of sweet release,
In silence, joy's embrace unwinds.

Soft whispers cradle tender dreams,
Euphoria drips like honey bright.
In tranquil depths, the spirit soars,
As shadows flee from morning light.

The heart beats slow, a steady drum,
In calm repose, we feel alive.
With every wave, sweet warmth returns,
A quiet flood, where passion thrives.

Let moments wash us, cleanse our souls,
In sacred stillness, sweet create.
For in the quiet, freedom flows,
Euphoria waits, no longer late.

The Quiet Ballet of Disarray

In shadows that tremble and sway,
The world spins in elegant fray.
Whispers of chaos dance round,
In silence, the lost can be found.

Mirrors reflect what's undone,
Footsteps of chaos, a work of art spun.
Grace in the flawed, a beauty so rare,
A gentle reminder to dance with care.

With every misstep, the heart learns to fly,
In the ballet of life, we stumble yet try.
Each twist and turn a lesson profound,
In the quiet of disarray, joy is unbound.

Embrace the dishevel, welcome the strife,
For beauty emerges from the chaos of life.
The quiet ballet holds treasures anew,
In moments of chaos, we find what is true.

Unraveled Threads of Solace

In the tapestry frayed, we discover,
Threads of our sorrows gently hover.
Each knot tells a tale, a soft whisper,
Of solace and strength, like a warm sister.

With hands worn and weary, we weave,
The fabric of hope that we grieve.
Fragments of dreams scattered about,
Together they whisper what life's all about.

Stitches of courage, patches of grace,
In this quilt of the heart, we find our place.
The colors of loss, a vibrant embrace,
Unraveled threads, we weave with a trace.

Bound by the stories of who we became,
In the silence, we heal through the pain.
Each thread a reminder, a promise endowed,
In unraveled solace, we stand unbowed.

Colorful Whispers in the Storm

When dark clouds gather, a fierce embrace,
Colorful whispers begin to trace.
Amidst the thunder's wild parade,
Hope dances lightly, never afraid.

Raindrops splatter like paint on the ground,
A symphony of hues in chaos resound.
Each flash of lightning, a brushstroke bright,
Illuminating shadows in the night.

The winds carry secrets of worlds yet unseen,
In every gust, vibrant dreams glean.
As the storm rages, hearts find their song,
In colorful whispers, we all belong.

Embrace the tempest, let colors collide,
In the heart of the storm, let your spirit reside.
For after the fury, the skies will be clear,
And in colorful whispers, hope will be near.

Breathing in Fractured Patterns

In fractured patterns, our souls entwine,
Breathing in chaos, a rhythm divine.
Each crack tells a story, a hidden refrain,
In the art of the broken, beauty remains.

Life's mosaic lies bare in the light,
With jagged edges, we find our flight.
Embracing the shards of hopes once bright,
We breathe deep the fragments of night.

In the silence, creations emerge,
Breathing in laughter, the heart learns to surge.
Discovering strength in what's torn,
From madness, new dreams are reborn.

So let us find solace in what we proclaim,
In breathing the fractured, we aren't the same.
For in every broken piece, love can be found,
Breathing in patterns where hope will astound.

Enigmas Wrapped in Soft Clamor

In shadows deep, the whispers twine,
Curved secrets dance, a velvet line.
With every breath, the night unfolds,
A story spun in threads of gold.

Beneath the stars, where silence sings,
Time weaves through invisible strings.
Each heartbeat hums a silent tune,
In mysteries held by the silver moon.

An echo plays on tender dreams,
Soft clamor wraps like gentle seams.
In quiet moments, truths collide,
As hearts open wide, let worlds confide.

Through veils of doubt, the light flows in,
Each enigma's breath, a hidden grin.
Awake in the night, we search anew,
Wrapped in clamor, the old feels true.

Feathers in the Eye of the Storm

In tempest's heart, the stillness breathes,
Feathers drift where chaos weaves.
A delicate dance on winds that howl,
In the eye of the storm, serenity's prowl.

Lightning strikes, but here it's calm,
A whisper floats, like a healing balm.
Nature's fury, yet peace remains,
As fleeting moments break the chains.

Through shadows cast by thundering skies,
A bright feather flits, the hope that flies.
In the swirling dust, a glimmer bright,
A promise held in the darkest night.

Catch the flutter, a gentle sign,
In wild turmoil, let love align.
Against the storm, the quiet grows,
Feathers whisper what the heart knows.

Whispers of Fractured Light

Through shattered beams, the colors play,
Whispers of light, an intricate ballet.
In fractured hues, a tale is spun,
Of shadows mingling, two as one.

A flicker here, a shimmer there,
Echoed glances in the cool night air.
Moments captured, suspended flight,
Dance with the whispers of fractured light.

Illuminated dreams cast on the ground,
In silent echoes, lost is found.
Every fragment holds a spark,
Guiding souls through the endless dark.

In the mosaic of day's demise,
Whispers of truth reflect the skies.
Through broken prisms, we find our way,
In splintered light, we learn to stay.

Echoes in a Shattered Silence

In the stillness, cracks appear,
A silence thick, yet whispers near.
Echoes linger, soft and low,
In shattered silence, feelings flow.

Each breath a ripple, spread like light,
An unseen touch in the quiet night.
Memories dance on fragile wings,
In the void, distant laughter rings.

Through cracks of time, shadows plead,
A chorus forms, a haunting bead.
In every silence, a story thrives,
Echoes weave what the heart derives.

So listen close, let echoes guide,
The beauty found in worlds untried.
For in fragments, whispers remain,
In shattered silence, we feel the gain.

Milton Keynes UK
Ingram Content Group UK Ltd.
UKHW030750121124
451094UK00013B/813